The Daemonic Companion

Creating Daemonic Entities to Do Your Will

Copyright information

Kadmon, Baal

The Daemonic Companion – Creating Daemonic Entities to Do Your Will

–1st ed

Printed in the United States of America

Cover image: #79594691 ⌐ igorigorevich - Fotolia.com

Book Cover Design: Baal Kadmon

Warning

Proceed at your own risk.

Other Books By The Author

The Mantra Magick Series:

VASHIKARAN MAGICK - LEARN THE DARK
MANTRAS OF SUBJUGATION
Kali Mantra Magick: Summoning The Dark Powers of Kali
Ma
Seed Mantra Magick: Master The Primordial Sounds of The
universe
Chakra Mantra Magick: Tap Into The Magick Of Your
Chakras

The Scared Names Series:

THE 72 NAMES OF GOD - THE 72 KEYS OF
TRANSFORMATION
THE 72 ANGELS OF THE NAME - CALLING ON THE 72
ANGELS OF GOD
THE 99 NAMES OF ALLAH - ACQUIRING THE 99
DIVINE QUALITIES OF GOD
THE HIDDEN NAMES OF GENESIS - TAP INTO THE
HIDDEN POWER OF MANIFESTATION
THE 72 DEMONS OF THE NAME: CALLING UPON THE
GREAT DEMONS OF THE NAME

Magick Of the Saints Series

Mary Magick: Calling Forth The Divine Mother For Help
The Magick of Saint Expedite: Tap Into the Truly
Miraculous Power of Saint Expedite

Ouija Board Magic Series

Ouija Board Magick – Archangel Edition _ Communicate
and Harness the Power of the Archangels

Crystal Magick Mantra Series

Moldavite Magick – Tap into the Stone of Transformation

Supernatural Attainments Series

Tap Into the Power Of the Chant – Attaining Supernatural Abilities Using

Mantras

Introduction

As you may know from my other books; I am a practitioner and writer on all matters of the occult. I do not belong to any school or order. I do not wear silly robes and paraphernalia, I don't have a silly title … (those are all distractions by the way). If I you want a title and a robe you can role-play Dungeons and Dragons or go to Dragoncon or other CON… I am also a solo practitioner. That said, being solo allows me to explore the spiritual realms without being encumbered by anyone or anything, I am not bound by any rules. I practice fully knowing the benefits and risks involved. It is this freedom that allows me to write about these things and to try them FIRST HAND. It is in this spirit that I write this book.

What you are about to read is not for the faint of heart. You will be creating a powerful spiritual entity. An entity that will know you better than you know yourself. It will know all your secrets, your weaknesses and your strengths. It will also be your servant. It will do whatever you tell it to do. Both good and ill. Although it is you who will create it, its energy and life force traces back deep into primordial time. People throughout history and even to this day call upon these entities for help. They aren't quite Gods, they aren't quite angels. They are Daemons, entities that live between the veil of the spirit and the earth, between the mundane and the esoteric. They are self-existent and yet created by all of us. Many use Daemons, yet do not know that they do so.

In this book you will learn how to create AND or tap into benign and malevolent Daemons. As I said before, this isn't for the faint of heart. You will be creating a being of immense power that will serve you. With that said, let us delve a bit into the history of what Daemons are. Additional note, I will be using the spelling Daemon and Daimon interchangeably.

What Are Daemons?

As I stated previously, Daemons have been used since the beginning of time to help or harm. Although the word Daemon has transformed to mean "Demon" in the west, they are, in fact not demons, although some can be malevolent. (A Very Small Fraction of the passages below are excerpted from my book: 72 Demons of the Name)

In ancient Greece, daemons were not considered evil. In fact, they were considered spirits or divine powers. Ancient Greece thought them spirits of inspiration and goodness as in the Greek word "EuDAIMONia" which means "good spiritedness" or "happiness" as it is often translated. It light of this, it is hard to believe that this word would so transform to mean something evil in the western tradition. Daemons became demons once Christianity became popular in Rome. As you may know, the Christian belief which was derived from the Jewish one that pagan idols and statutes of any kind were presentations of evil, especially those of ancient gods. That is because the Romans and Greeks believed that Daemons inhabited those statues. As Robin Lane Fox Put it "Like pagans, Christians still sensed and saw the gods and their power, and as something, they had to assume, lay behind it, by an easy traditional shift of opinion they turned these pagan *daimones* into malevolent 'demons', the troupe of Satan..... Far into the Byzantine period Christians eyed their cities' old pagan statuary as a seat of the demons' presence. It was no longer beautiful, it was infested. - Robin Lane Fox, Pagans And Christians 1989, P. 137.

In the Greek translation of the bible called the "Septuagint" the word daemon first became associated with evil because it was associated with the gods of the ancient Semitic religions. This later passed on to other translations and eventually took on its evil definition and called "demon".

In ancient Greece, (There is also evidence that daimons were used the Minoans and Mycenaeans as well circa (1500-1100 BC). mainly at the hands of philosophers like Plato, daemons were classified into 2 categories; Those with Beneficent intent and those with malevolent intent. The ones that were "good" were called Eudaimon or "noble in spirit" and the "evil" ones were known as Kakodaimon which literally translates into "Malevolent Spirit". As I stated above, they aren't technically angels or demons in the proper sense. However, they can be loosely associated to the wests conception of angels and demons. Angels and demons are the only real comparison that can be made. The Western traditions don't really have daemons in the way the ancient Greeks viewed them to be. I think a better comparison would the Jinn of Arabic lore. They are "Genies" for lack of a better term.

It is these 2 classes of Daemon we will be most interested in. In the next 2 chapters I will briefly explain the differences between the Eudaimon and the Kakodaimon.

The Eudaimon

In ancient Greek Mythology Eudaimon was mostly associated with protecting fields of grain and vineyards, but it was also considered a companion spirit or "Familiar". It was known to help bestow knowledge, wisdom, good fortune and good luck to the person they were attached to. A person who had a Eudaimon was considered very fortunate.

Eudaimons are considered excellent guides and counselors. Some who have created them say they hear whispers in their ear from them, giving them guidance as to what to do or say in any given situation. It was believed that Socrates had a Eudaimon daemon that would guide him in his conduct and warn him of physical threats and misguided thoughts. Socrates himself said that his Eudaimon was very accurate in divining the future, even more accurate than the other methods used at the time.

A particular Eudaimon named Agathodaemon in Greek Mythology was the companion of the Goddess Tyche Agathe who also is associated with good fortune.

Some say that Eudaimon is a singular being and as mentioned above, is a class of daemons. The understanding is that it is a class of daemons since it is said that a person who had a Eudaimon would be a person who had achieved Eudaimonia which means "good spiritedness" or "happiness". The Daemon would literally be incorporated into the persons essence or aura I guess you could say. Since more than one person embodied these qualities it is felt it represented a spirit familiar or companion helper.

Further proof that it was a class of daemons is that Greek families always called upon it in private. Right before every meal, they would pour a few drops of wine to it. Often offerings were left for the daimon.

In this book we will discuss how to call upon and create Eudaimons. You can use them for whatever you like. In this book, however, we will use it to help you with protection, Riches and love. At the end of these rituals, you will need to give an offering. I will discuss that in a future chapter.

The Kakodaimon

In Greek, (KAKOS DAIMON) or "evil spirit" (Approximate meaning). Throughout the history of this daemon, it is said that it has shape-shifting abilities and had the ability to infiltrate a person's dreams and cause nightmares. It also had the power to "possess" a person if they did not have the ability to handle it. Its interesting to note that in modern psychology, the condition in which a person believes he or she is possessed by an evil spirit is called "Cacodemonia".

As the Eudaimon, the Kacodaimon is a kind of familiar. It was used to cause misfortune on others BUT also deceive the very person they were attached to. In that way they can be dangerous.

Kakodaimon are considered powerful agents of deception and malice. Some who have created them say they see them in the shadows or in the corner of their eyes. Often giving guidance which is often malevolent in nature and tailored to the person's request.

As the Eudaimon, the Kakodaimon is a singular being and as mentioned above, is a class of daemons. The understanding is that it is a class of daemons.

As you can see, not a lot is known about Daemons in general, but they do exist from the countless people who have used them. If you do a search online you will find many forums discussing the use of daemons. In this book we will discuss how to call upon and create Kaokdaemons. You can use them for whatever dark ritual you will cast. In this book, however, we will use it to help you with the subjugation of your enemies, the binding of people to your will and to create storms. At the end of these rituals, you will need to give an offering. I will discuss that in the next chapter. This is very important, a Kakodaimon will most definitely turn on you without an offering. In this next chapter will discuss offerings.

Making an Offering

Throughout ancient history we have heard of the many traditions that required blood sacrifices to be made to appease a God or a demon. The daemons are no exception. **HOWEVER, we will not be making blood sacrifices and we do not need to kill anything.**

The offerings for the Eudaimon and the Kakodaimons are very different. We discuss the Kakodaimons first

Offering to a Kakodaimon

You must make an offering to them. They are a give and take energy. If you do not give, you cannot take. Even worse, if you do not give, they will take from you something. So it is very important to offer them something in return.

Since we are not in 2000 BC, we cannot offer a blood sacrifice to the kakodaimons. However, we can do the next best thing. We can offer them something that was once alive or has life potential. This might sound very odd to you, but this is what I mean.

You can offer them a piece of meat. Any animal meat you can obtain from the supermarket. If you would rather not use meat, you can use an egg.

The meat is representative of something once alive and an egg contains the potential for life. I know this sounds awful, but this is how one appeases forces like these. Almost every book on magick omits this because they are afraid to say it. I am not afraid.

All you will need to do is offer one or the other of those above on a plate to the daimon, will get into this shortly.

Offering to a Eudaimon

Eudaimons are gentler and more loving than the kakodaimons. All you will need to offer them is a single flower or even a bouquet if you like. They do not require anything else. Simple enough I suppose. In the next chapter we will discuss basic objects you will need in order to make the rituals more effective.

Things You Will Need

Here are a few things I think are needed to work with daemons. Of course, you do not really need these but I feel they will help you anchor the energy in your mind.

1. Frankincense and Myrrh: This Incense is a wonderful sacred fragrance and was once more precious

than gold. It was so valuable that people would rather it than gold itself. I find the fragrance holy and

fitting for this work.

2. Candles: (Please note you can buy any kind of candle you like, they don't have to be chimes or

votive. I just happen to like the ones I provided here)

Red Chime Candles: This color is quite powerful. We will use this for the Love daemons.

Gold Candles: This candle will be used for the riches daemon. Many occultists will tell you

to use green, but this has been a long-held misconception. The only reason why people have said to use green is because it's the color of money. The thing is, it's only the color of money in the USA and maybe

a few notes here and there of other nations. They don't call the dollar "greenback" for nothing. Green is

not a color that is truly indicative money. Gold is though, Gold is UNIVERSALLY known to be a signifier of

wealth both in ancient times and present. If you have been using Green for your money rituals, now you

know to use gold instead. It is much more effective.

 White Candles: White is for purity and protection, we will use it for our protection ritual.

 Black Candles: These candles will be used for all rituals we perform with the kakodaimons.

3. The offerings to the daemons: Piece of meat or an egg for the kakodaimon and a flower or flowers for the eudaimon.

As you can see, these few items are not complicated, as I mentioned, you can use all of these or none, Only the offerings are truly mandatory.

The Steps To Creating a Daemon

In order to tap into the powers of these daemons we need to follow a few VERY SIMPLE steps. Unlike other books on this topic, we will not be doing anything elaborate or time consuming. These energies are spiritual and are not subject to human temperaments. It is silly to assume that we need to cast circles and point to the various directions in order to summon them. Do you really think a circle of salt with a few names of God are going to contain these energies? It won't. Most rituals are used to Anchor the mind but they do nothing to the spirits. In the sessions that will follow, we will create daemons for subjugation of your enemies, the binding of people to your will and to create storms as well as protection, Riches and love. You can create a single daemon if you like, but I will separate it out for the sake of ease and understanding. As a side note, you will only need to do these rituals once.

Here are the steps:

1. Light the incense and the candles.

2. State out loud or in silence the intent of the daemon you will be creating.

3. Place the offer of the Meat, Egg or flower/s on the altar. In the center preferably.

4. Say the specific prayer I will itemize for each session

5. Sit quiet and allow the daemon to show itself in your mind or perhaps in front of you.

6. Give it a name or let it give you its name.

7. Tell the Daemon to do what you created it to do. You can say the prayer above again if you like. But at this point, it is under your control.

8. Finish with saying "Let it Be done"

9. You may cast the offerings to nature and let nature take its course on them.

10. Make sure to remember the name of the daimon, you will simply need to mention the name in your mind or out load in order to call it from now on.

Creating a Kakodaemon for subjugation of your enemies

1. Light the incense and the black candle.

2. State out loud or in silence the enemies you wish to subjugate

3. Place the offer of the Meat, or Egg the altar. In the center preferably.

4. Say this prayer:

"Kakodaimon I call you forth and create you to do my bidding. Seek the one who wishes to harm me and subjugate them to me. Make it so they will no longer have any control to harm me. Come to my bidding, to subjugate my enemy. No one can harm me, by your power. So mote it be"

5. Sit quiet and allow the daemon to show itself in your mind or perhaps in front of you.

6. Give it a name or let it give you its name

7. Tell the Daemon again to do what you created it to do. You can say the prayer above again if you like. But at this point, it is under your control.

8. Finish with saying "Let it Be done"

9. You may cast the offerings to nature and let nature take its course on them.

10. Make sure to remember the name of the daimon, you will simply need to mention the name in your mind or out load in order to call it from now on.

Thus concludes the ritual.

Creating a Kakodaemon for The binding of people

1. Light the incense and the black candle.

2. State out loud or in silence the person or persons you wish to gain control over. They may not be enemies per se but people you want to control for whatever purpose you desire.

3. Place the offer of the Meat, or Egg the altar. In the center preferably.

4. Say this prayer:

"Kakodaimon I call you forth and create you to bind _____. Seek out _____ and place them under my control. Make it so they will no longer have any control save what I tell them to do. Come to my bidding, to bind _____. By your power. So mote it be"

5. Sit quiet and allow the daemon to show itself in your mind or perhaps in front of you.

6. Give it a name or let it give you its name

7. Tell the Daemon again to do what you created it to do. You can say the prayer above again if you like. But at this point, it is under your control.

8. Finish with saying "Let it Be done"

9. You may cast the offerings to nature and let nature take its course on them.

10. Make sure to remember the name of the daimon, you will simply need to mention the name in your mind or out load in order to call it from now on.

Thus concludes the ritual.

Creating a Kakodaemon to produce violent storms

1. Light the incense and the black candle.

2. State out loud or in silence that you wish to have control over the tempest.

3. Place the offer of the Meat, or Egg the altar. In the center preferably.

4. Say this prayer:

"Kakodaimon I call you forth and create you , give to me the power to control the Earth, Air, Water and Fire. Place these mighty powers of nature under my control. Make it so that when I call upon you, you will manipulate the forces of nature to do my bidding. By your power. So mote it be"

5. Sit quiet and allow the daemon to show itself in your mind or perhaps in front of you.

6. Give it a name or let it give you its name

7. Tell the Daemon again to do what you created it to do. You can say the prayer above again if you like. But at this point, it is under your control.

8. Finish with saying "Let it Be done"

9. You may cast the offerings to nature and let nature take its course on them.

10. Make sure to remember the name of the daimon, you will simply need to mention the name in your mind or out load in order to call it from now on.

Thus concludes the ritual.

Creating a Eudaemon for protection

1. Light the incense and the white candle.

2. State out loud or in silence your need for protection, you can be as specific as you like.

3. Place the offer of the flower or flowers on the altar. In the center preferably.

4. Say this prayer:

"Eudaimon I call you forth and create you, my home/body/mind is my abode and castle. You are its shield. I send you forth to protect me. Protect me from all people or things that may wish to or accidently do me harm. By your power. So mote it be"

5. Sit quiet and allow the daemon to show itself in your mind or perhaps in front of you.

6. Give it a name or let it give you its name

7. Tell the Daemon again to do what you created it to do. You can say the prayer above again if you like. But at this point, it is under your control.

8. Finish with saying "Let it Be done"

9. You may cast the offerings to nature and let nature take its course on them.

10. Make sure to remember the name of the daimon, you will simply need to mention the name in your mind or out load in order to call it from now on.

Thus concludes the ritual.

Creating a Eudaemon for Riches

1. Light the incense and the Gold candle.

2. State out loud or in silence your need for riches, you can be as broad or specific as you like.

3. Place the offer of the flower or flowers on the altar. In the center preferably.

4. Say this prayer:

"Eudaimon I call you forth and create you, you of benevolent heart, please bring me luck and fortune. Enrich my life with riches and prosperity. By my bidding may it be so. By your power it will be done. So mote it be"

5. Sit quiet and allow the daemon to show itself in your mind or perhaps in front of you.

6. Give it a name or let it give you its name

7. Tell the Daemon again to do what you created it to do. You can say the prayer above again if you like. But at this point, it is under your control.

8. Finish with saying "Let it Be done"

9. You may cast the offerings to nature and let nature take its course on them.

10. Make sure to remember the name of the daimon, you will simply need to mention the name in your mind or out load in order to call it from now on.

Thus concludes the ritual.

Creating a Eudaemon for Love

1. Light the incense and the red candle.

2. State out loud or in silence your need for love, it can be either the love of someone specific or to attract love in general,

3. Place the offer of the flower or flowers on the altar. In the center preferably.

4. Say this prayer:

"Eudaimon I call you forth and create you, you of benevolent heart and loving , please bring into my live love (or love of _____). Enrich my heart and mind with love and passion. By my bidding may it be so. By your power it will be done. So mote it be"

5. Sit quiet and allow the daemon to show itself in your mind or perhaps in front of you.

6. Give it a name or let it give you its name

7. Tell the Daemon again to do what you created it to do. You can say the prayer above again if you like. But at this point, it is under your control.

8. Finish with saying "Let it Be done"

9. You may cast the offerings to nature and let nature take its course on them.

10. Make sure to remember the name of the daimon, you will simply need to mention the name in your mind or out load in order to call it from now on.

Thus concludes the ritual.

Conclusion

We have come to the end of this text. I know it might not seem like much, but what you have just learned here will allow you to create your own daemons. Often we are beguiled by overly complex methods of magic. We think " if it is elaborate and complex, it must be good." This, my friend, is not the case. Our ability to create daemons is meant to be easy, not hard. Anyone who tells you that we must work and toil in order to connect to create spiritual beings is not telling you the truth. Just on a logical basis alone it doesn't make sense to have to toil to BE the creator that you are.

I am confident that by simply doing these rituals with the daemons, you will gain great benefit.

Disclaimer

The Information in this book is for educational purposes only and not for treatment, diagnosis or prescription of any diseases or life situations. All advice is for educational purposes only. The Author and the publisher of this book are in no way liable for any misuse of the material. In addition, you agree to purchase this book as is. I Cannot Promise you results. You will not hold Baal Kadmon or his affiliates liable for any harm this book may cause you.

37101485R00022

Made in the USA
San Bernardino, CA
10 August 2016